When Bill Gates Memorized an Encyclopedia

by Mark Weakland

illustrated by Jeff Ebbeler

PICTURE WINDOW BOOKS
a capstone imprint

The ASR-33 Teletype machine whirred and clicked.
It could send and receive typed messages. Bill Gates
couldn't keep his hands off the keyboard. At 13 years
old, Bill was obsessed with computers. He read
books about them. He spent hours writing programs.
**"To this day it still thrills me to know that if I
can get the program right it will always work
perfectly, every time, just the way I told it to,"**
Bill said later.

Today Bill Gates still has the qualities he had as a boy.
He is curious and competitive. He is focused and
creative. And he still loves computers! Bill used these
traits to build one of the most successful companies
in the world.

Bill Gates was born October 28, 1955. His full name was William Henry Gates III. His family lived in a big house in Seattle, Washington.

Bill's father and grandfather were named William too. This worried his grandmother. "Having so many Bills in one family is confusing," she said. "He needs a nickname. I think you should call him Trey." Trey is the number three card in a card deck. The nickname stuck.

As a young boy, Bill saw his parents being creative. He saw them working and learning too. His father studied to become a lawyer. His mother worked to raise Bill and his sister, Kristi. She also created new traditions for her family.

Each Christmas, Bill's grandparents bought matching pajamas for everyone in the family. They thought it was funny to hang them right on the tree. Bill's mother created a new custom with the clothes. Every Christmas morning, the family put on their new PJs. Then they gathered at the tree and opened their gifts.

Another tradition the Gates family created was summer vacation. Each year they went to a resort called Cheerio. Other families joined them to swim, picnic, and play games. The mothers' favorite game was "Round Rock." The kids were challenged to find the roundest rock.

"How about this one?" asked Bill.

"Hmm, I don't know," said his mother. "I think you can find a rounder one, Trey." Bill sprinted away in search of another rock. The kids never knew that their mothers' goal was to sit and relax.

Mrs. Gates made her children's life at home interesting. There was discussion at dinner. There were theater skits to act out and board games to play. Bill was really good at Monopoly.

There were competitions, even about the dishes. Games were after dinner. The winner didn't have to help wash and put away the plates. Bill wanted to win. "Trey, what you are learning now will help you succeed in the future," said his dad.

Bill was even competitive about reading. Every year his teachers held a contest. The goal was to read the most books on the summer reading list. Bill loved to learn, and he loved to compete. "Look, Dad," he said. "I won the contest . . . again!"

But reading wasn't just about being the best. Bill was also naturally curious. At the library, he checked out mounds of books. He read them quickly and then asked to go back for more. Bill read everywhere. He even read at the dinner table. "Put it away, Trey," said his mother. "It's not polite to read at the table."

Sales and business were also on young Bill's mind. To make money, his Cub Scout troop sold nuts for the holidays. Groups of scouts competed to see who could raise the most cash. Bill spent hours knocking on doors, asking people if they would buy nuts. He listened to their answers. He noted why some people bought nuts and others didn't.

Everyone knew Bill was very smart. When he was eight, he read a whole set of encyclopedias. Because he had an excellent memory, he could recall many facts. But he knew that to get ahead, he'd have to study too.

Reverend Turner was the leader of Bill's church. Every year he had a challenge. Any kid who could memorize a long Bible verse would win dinner in Seattle's famous Space Needle. Bill learned 2,000 words. Then he recited them with no mistakes. No one had ever given such a perfect performance.

Bill wasn't perfect in everything, though. Like many kids, he was a "know it all." And he was strong-willed. When he was 12 years old, he acted rude, especially toward his mother. He argued with her about everything. "Why do I have to keep my room clean?" he yelled. "And what's so bad about biting pencils?"

A counselor gave his parents advice. "Why not back off? Ease up on him a bit." Taking the advice, Bill and Mary Gates enrolled their son in a private school.

"We want you to have more freedom, Trey," they said. "In return, we expect good behavior and respect."

19

Lakeside School gave Bill more than freedom. It also gave him access to computers. In the 1960s, it was rare for a school to have even one computer. Schools had to raise money to buy a keyboard and printer called a terminal. It connected to a giant mainframe computer kept in another building. Schools had to buy computer time.

The computer fascinated Bill. He spent hours on it, learning how to write programs. The first one he wrote allowed a person to play tic-tac-toe against the computer. **"Of course, in those days we were just goofing around, or so we thought,"** he said later. **"But the toy we had—well, it turned out to be some toy."**

Bill and his friend Paul Allen spent so much time on Lakeside School's terminal that they soon used up all of the school's computer time. But the boys were smart, and sneaky. To get more time, they changed the usage record.

When the computer company found out, it banned them from the computer. But later, they struck a deal. In return for unlimited time, Bill and Paul looked for computer "bugs" and told the company about them.

"The school could have shut down the terminal, or they could have tightly regulated who got to use it," Bill said later. **"Instead, they opened it up."**

Later, Bill formed a business with Paul. They called it Traf-O-Data. Traf-O-Data was a piece of computer equipment. It created a graph that showed how road traffic flowed, hour by hour. After showing his parents, Bill convinced City of Seattle employees to come to his house and see it in person. It did not go well. The Traf-O-Data failed.

Bill ran into the kitchen. **"Mom, Mom!"** he called. **"Come out here and tell them that the machine really works!"**

In the end, the Traf-O-Data worked. Bill and Paul sold it for $20,000. Paul, who was older than Bill, wanted his friend to quit high school and form a company with him. But Bill's parents said no. "Bill, you are going to graduate."

Bill graduated from Lakeside School in 1973 and got into Harvard University. He studied law, just like his father. But he still spent a lot of time using computers and writing code. With Paul, he started a company called Microsoft. Soon Bill would find success doing what he loved.

Afterword

In 1980, Bill Gates and Paul Allen purchased software for one of the world's first personal computers. The program had more than 300 bugs. Gates and Allen quickly fixed them. After that, the program worked perfectly.

Their company, Microsoft, provided the operating system for every new personal computer made by IBM. Gates and Allen sold their program for a large fee and they kept the software copyright. When the personal computer market took off, Microsoft sold the program to other computer makers. Soon, Microsoft was the operating system in most of the world's computers. Later, Microsoft created other programs, such as Word and PowerPoint. From software sales and the value of his company's stock, Bill Gates became the richest man in the world. Soon people, including his mother, urged Bill to give much of his immense wealth to charity.

In 1994, he married Melinda French. In 2000, they formed the Bill and Melinda Gates Foundation. The foundation gives money to many causes, from combatting global climate change to curing diseases like polio and malaria. Today the Bill and Melinda Gates Foundation is one of the world's largest charitable organizations. Bill Gates has donated more than $28 billion of his own money to charity.

Glossary

competitive – very eager to win, succeed, or excel

data – information or facts

encyclopedia – a book that gives information on subjects that are usually arranged in alphabetical order

mainframe – a large computer used for storing and processing data

operating system – the software that allows a user to run applications on a computer

skit – a short play that is often funny

software – the programs that tell the hardware of the computer what to do

terminal – the hardware used to enter data into a computer

Read More

Gregory, Josh. *Bill and Melinda Gates.* A True Book. New York: Children's Press, 2013.

Roza, Greg. *Bill and Melinda Gates.* Making a Difference: Leaders Who Are Changing the World. New York: Rosen Publishing Group, 2015.

Strand, Jennifer. *Bill Gates.* Zoom in on Technology Pioneers. Minneapolis: Abdo Zoom, 2017.

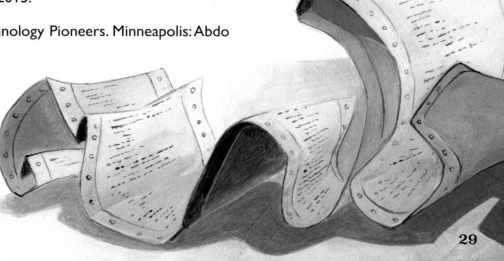

Critical Thinking Questions

1. What childhood character traits and abilities did Bill Gates have that helped him become the creator of one of the world's most successful companies?

2. What skills did Bill learn as a child that helped him succeed as an adult? Use text evidence to support your answer.

3. Construct a timeline of Bill Gates' life, from the time he was born to the present year.

4. People other than Bill Gates and Paul Allen were important in creating the personal computer. Ask an adult to help you look up information about Steve Jobs and Stephen Wozniak on the Internet. How was what they did similar to what Gates and Allen did? How was it different?

Internet Sites

FactHound offers a safe, fun way to find Internet sites related to this book. All of the sites on FactHound have been researched by our staff.

Here's all you do:

Visit *www.facthound.com*

Type in this code: 9781515830405

Check out projects, games and lots more at
www.capstonekids.com

Other Titles in this Series

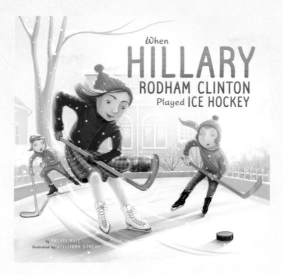

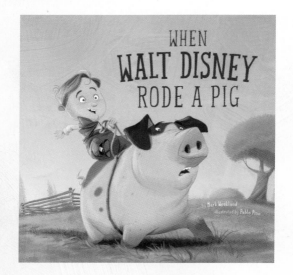

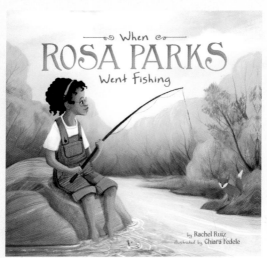

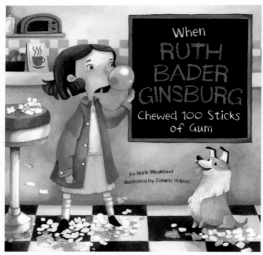

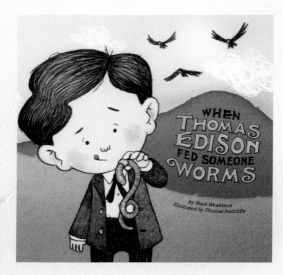

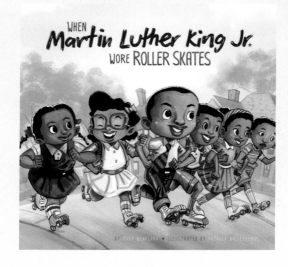

Special thanks to our adviser for his advice and expertise:
Miles Smayling, Minnsota State University, Mankato
College of Business, Department of Management

Editor: Mari Bolte
Designer: Ashlee Suker
Creative Director: Nathan Gassman
Production Specialist: Kris Wilfahrt
The illustrations in this book were created digitally.

Editor's Note: Direct quotations are indicated by **bold** words.

Direct quotations are found on the following pages:

page 2, line 6: Gates, Bill. *The Road Ahead*. Viking Penguin,
a division of Penguin Books USA Inc., 1995 page 2

page 20, line 9: Ibid.

page 23, line 9: Gates, Bill. [2005] "Bill Gates — Lakeside School (speech).
https://www.gatesfoundation.org/media-center/speeches/2005/09/bill-gates-lakeside-school

page 25, line 1: Gates, William H. *Showing Up for Life: Thoughts on the Gifts
of a Lifetime*. Broadway Books, 2009 page 1

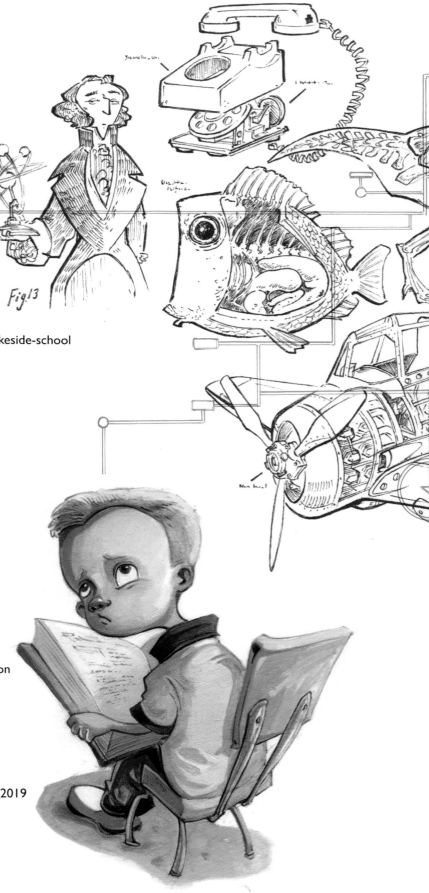

Picture Window Books are published by Capstone,
1710 Roe Crest Drive, North Mankato, Minnesota 56003
www.mycapstone.com

Library of Congress Cataloging-in-Publication Data
Names: Weakland, Mark, author. | Ebbeler, Jeffrey, illustrator.
Title: When Bill Gates memorized an encyclopedia / by Mark Weakland ;
    illustrated by Jeffrey Ebbeler.
Description: North Mankato, Minnesota : Capstone, [2019] | Series: Nonfiction
    picture. books leaders doing headstands | Audience: Ages 6-12.
Identifiers: LCCN 2018018820 (print) | LCCN 2018020113 (ebook) |
ISBN 9781515830535 (eBook PDF) | ISBN 9781515830405 (hardcover) |
ISBN 9781515830498 (paperback)
Subjects: LCSH: Gates, Bill, 1955—Childhood and youth—Juvenile literature.
    | Businesspeople—United States—Biography—Juvenile literature. |
    Computer software industry—United States—Juvenile literature.
Classification: LCC HD9696.63.U62 (ebook) | LCC HD9696.63.U62 G3776 2019
    (print) | DDC 338.7/61004092 [B]—dc23
LC record available at https://lccn.loc.gov/2018018820

Printed in the United States of America.
PA021